MW01617893
Ole Miss
CHAMPIONS
NCAA
NATIONAL CHAMPION

OLE MISS: 2022 BASEBALL NATIONAL

CHAMPIONS

THE NAUTILUS PUBLISHING COMPANY

PHOTOGRAPHY EDITOR: JOSHUA T. MCCOY
WRITERS: JEFF ROBERSON, MITCH PRAXL & ALEX SIMS
EDITOR: NEIL WHITE

NCAA
ONAL CHAMPION
25

FOREWORD
BY TIM ELKO

On Monday, June 14, 2021, after a second loss to Arizona in the Tucson Super Regional tournament, our team flew back to Mississippi and boarded a bus for Oxford. When the team bus arrived at Swayze Field, our hitting coach Mike Clement walked to the back of the bus where the hitters were sitting.

Coach Clem looked around at us. "Hey," he said, "I know this sucks."

We'd all felt the disappointment of the last three years — a Super Regional loss to Arkansas in Fayetteville in 2019, a shortened 2020 season where Ole Miss was leading the nation in home runs, and in 2021, another Super Regional loss to Arizona.

"If we keep on this journey, if we keep working hard," Coach Clement said, "we're going to win a Super Regional and get over the hump. We're gonna get to Omaha and we're going to do this thing."

• • •

We started the 2022 season with a record of 13-2 and we were ranked #1 in the polls. But then, like sometimes happens in baseball, we hit a slump. We lost games we could have won. We didn't hit or pitch or field like we knew we could.

We went 7-14 in SEC play in March and April. Coach Bianco knew we needed something — something to help us all regain our confidence, a belief in ourselves.

Before the Missouri series began on May 6, 2022, Coach asked former major leaguer and Ole Miss alum Chris Coghlan to speak to the team.

Chris stood before all the players and challenged each of us. He challenged us to ignore the noise. He challenged us to forget our record and past shortcomings. He challenged us to believe with conviction — in ourselves, in our teammates, and in the notion that every time we stepped onto the field, we were going to win.

And then, Chris challenged us to go for the national championship. Not only did he challenge us to go for the national championship, but he challenged us to believe with conviction that the national championship was ours for the taking.

This idea of belief that Chris presented hit me a little differently that day. Just a few weeks earlier, after losing the series to Mississippi State at home, God had told me in prayer that I needed to "Believe." That was the one word He continued to put in the back of my head. So, as many things that happen in the hand of God, this speech from Chris did not come as a huge surprise to me, as this coincidence of this topic seemed more like a reassurance of what God had told me just a few weeks earlier. It was from there on out that I knew that God's hand was on this situation, and that "Belief" was the answer.

After hearing God's demand to believe and Chris' speech to the team, we changed. We finished the season winning 18 of 22 games, including 10 of 11 in the post-season, and we did bring home a national title.

The Ole Miss fans returned with enthusiasm, too. They followed us by the tens of thousands because they wanted to be part of this remarkable tale — to witness the unfolding of our most improbable, inspired sports story. They brought Oxford to Nebraska. They made it difficult for opposing teams in Omaha, just like they do at Swayze. They showed the nation what it meant to be real college baseball fans.

This book — *Ole Miss: 2022 Baseball National Champions* — chronicles the highs and lows of our sensational 2022 season. As you turn the pages, read the narrative, and view the stunning collection of photographs, I hope you will be as captivated as you were during the season.

• • •

Every great story has conflict, drama, tension, a few good laughs, colorful characters, plots and subplots, and points in the plot where all hope seems to be lost. These stories also have a strong beginning and a knockout ending.

Our season had all this and more.

After the final game in Omaha, I told a reporter, "The story of our season is going to be told for years and years to come."

This I believe with conviction.

A DIFFERENT PATH
BY COACH MIKE BIANCO

The 2022 Ole Miss baseball team was similar to a lot of teams I've coached over the years —a super talented team that started the season believing it had a shot to get to Omaha and compete for a national championship. We've had a lot of teams like that here. But this one traveled a different path.

Not that the other teams didn't face adversity, not that they didn't have a bad weekend or two, because they did. Even the 2014 team that went to the College World Series had some tough weekends. We had ups and downs that season.

This year's path was obviously much different. This team's journey captured not only our fanbase but also baseball fans everywhere.

We got off to a great start. However, the Southeastern Conference has a way of humbling you. If you don't play well, you lose. We had a few weeks in the middle of the season where we struggled. Eventually, we started playing better, but we were still losing too many close games. To the players' credit, they hung in there.

ON LEVEL GROUND

Once we were selected for the NCAA Tournament, I didn't know how we would respond. In retrospect, we weren't climbing uphill anymore. We were 0-0 again. We were starting in the same position as every other team.

Once we got to level ground, a huge weight was lifted. That helped us not only play well but also play well consistently. Every pitch wasn't so pressure packed. Every at-bat didn't seem like the season was riding on it.

THE TURNAROUND

It's easy to look back and say the turnaround started with the sweep of Missouri at home in early May. Or the next weekend when we swept LSU in Baton Rouge. I thought we played well at home against Mississippi State and at Arkansas the two weekends before Missouri. We just didn't win those weekends. We weren't good enough. But we were close and playing better.

Sometimes when you're close and it doesn't go your way, you get those feelings of *It's just not meant to be*. Some teams do that. This team didn't. They continued to believe.

I never remember a time when I walked into a team meeting, or we started a game and I looked in the dugout, or I looked at their faces during practice and felt like we weren't going to win. When you're good and you believe in yourself and your teammates, you've always got a shot.

When our name was called for the NCAA Tournament on Memorial Day, I've never seen a team react the way I saw this team react. Emotionally. Excited. Fired up. Some years we knew we were hosting a regional and were just waiting to find out who we'd be playing. Without a doubt, this team's response was genuine — they were ready to play more baseball.

OTHER VOICES

Before the Missouri weekend, Chris Coghlan, who played here, was the National League Rookie of the Year in 2009, and played for years in the major league, spoke to our team. His message was what we needed at that time. Chris said ultimately the only goal that matters is to win a national championship. Everything else has been done at Ole Miss. *Can you win a national championship here this year?* he asked them. Their answer was *yes*.

Chris reminded the players that they had let other people steal their goals, that they'd let other people temper their expectations. And he told them shame on you for that, for letting others change your mindset. He told them that even where they were right then, and that was 7-14 in the SEC, they could still win a national championship.

I could see that his message resonated with the guys.

When we went to Miami for the Regional, one of my former teammates, Luis Garcia, spoke to the team. He owns a restaurant, we had a team meal there, and he was terrific when he talked to our team.

In Omaha, I said in the first pregame talk "If Chris Coghlan was here, he would say . . ." and then Chris walked in from the back and announced, "I am here."

The players — who had no idea Chris was in town — went crazy. And he had another great message for them.

Before our next game, I mentioned Luis Garcia again. The players started looking around for him. And although he wasn't in Omaha, he did send a video with another powerful message.

Sometimes it's good for players to hear other voices, and those were certainly good, perfectly timed messages for this team.

OVERWHELMING SUPPORT

Our fan base is remarkable. I know this from my 22 years here. But I'm still amazed at what winning this national championship means to so many of them.

The tremendous support of Ole Miss fans and the Ole Miss family, watching Rebel Nation show up in so many different ways, that's something that's been almost overwhelming. It touches your heart.

I knew our fans cared and would be excited by this team winning it all, but I didn't know they cared so deeply and would be this excited.

The crowds in Omaha continued to grow as the week went on. When we would leave the hotel, it seemed like there were thousands waiting to send us off. We felt their love, their support, and their desire for us to win.

When we arrived back in Oxford the day after we won the national championship, there were thousands in the Grove along the Walk of Champions. And 36 hours later we did the parade and there were thousands of people there. Then it hit me, we're going to the stadium and they're doing this celebration live on the SEC Network, and I'm thinking there won't be many people there. I figured everyone was along the parade route. But there they were — inside the stadium — another eight, ten, twelve thousand people.

A GREAT FAMILY

This national championship is also for the former players who have been through our program, for all who have ever worn the uniform. They are a part of this.

We have a great coaching staff and, of course, a lot of great players. They are like family.

And my own family, for them to allow me to do this for all these years is such a blessing. You don't get here by yourself. You don't get here without a great family.

This could have happened in other years with other teams, but for whatever reasons it didn't. For the players this year to continue to put the uniform on, to represent this great university, to play baseball like they did, is something special.

And all who came before them, every player who came so close to going all the way, and all who helped build this program deserve a part of this special season for Ole Miss baseball.

Nautilus Publishing, 426 S. Lamar Blvd., Suite 16, Oxford, MS 38655
Email: info@nautiluspublishing.com • Phone: 662-513-0159 • www.NautilusPublishing.com

Photography by Ole Miss Athletics Photography: Joshua T. McCoy, manager, Petre Thomas, Kiana Dale, Reed Jones, Bruce Newman, Jackson Newman
Text by Ole Miss Athletics/Jeff Roberson, Mitch Praxl, Alex Sims
Front cover design by Jeffrey Rose
Edited by Neil White

ISBN: 978-1-949455-34-2 • Printed in the United States of America

CONTENTS

Jack Washburn
pitching against ULM

THE ASCENT

FEBRUARY 18-MARCH 25, 2022

OPENING DAY

Since Coach Mike Bianco's arrival in Oxford in the Summer of 2000, Ole Miss students and Rebel baseball fans have become more and more engaged with and supportive of the program. That enthusiasm is never more evident than one week before opening day when students line up to claim their spots beyond the right field wall — where excitement is at a fever pitch, where cheers echo beyond the stadium, where home runs are celebrated with beverage showers while Ole Miss players round the bases.

Opening Day 2022 was even more special than usual for Bianco. He had just been named by USA Baseball as the manager of the 2022 Collegiate National Team.

"I am honored and humbled to be selected as the manager of the Collegiate National Team," said Bianco. "I coached the team as an assistant back in 2013, and it was one of those 'dream come true' scenarios. Anytime you can put 'USA' across your chest and represent your country, it is a special thing, and to do it again as the manager is a really cool feeling."

But before Bianco could focus any attention on the national team, he and his players faced another full season of Rebel baseball. In his twenty-one previous seasons leading the program, Bianco had delivered seventeen postseason appearances, including seven Super Regional berths and a trip to the College World Series in 2014. He had earned almost every Ole Miss baseball coaching record, and he stood at No. 3 all time in wins among SEC coaches.

Despite that success, Coach Bianco, his coaching staff, and the forty-one players on the Ole Miss roster understood there was unfinished business. And the path to completion ran through Omaha.

SO CLOSE, SO MANY TIMES

During the three years prior to the 2022 season, Ole Miss baseball maintained a lofty perch nationally. Following the 2019 season, the Rebels won a NCAA Regional at home, but lost a Super Regional at Arkansas. Ole Miss had one of the nation's best starts — 16-1 — in 2020 (they also led the nation in home runs with 37) and seemed poised for another run at the College World Series when the season was cut short by COVID. And in 2021, the Rebels won another Oxford Regional, beating Southern Miss in the finale to advance, but the Rebels lost again in the Super Regional in Arizona (both USM and Arizona would play a role in the Rebels' 2022 postseason campaign).

GREAT, AS PREDICTED

During the 2022 preseason, the Rebels were ranked in the top five in the nation. Ole Miss came out in 2022 swinging. The Rebels opened the season against Charleston Southern (coached by former Ole Miss player and assistant coach, Marc MacMillan). The Buccaneer squad was no match for Ole Miss. The Rebels swept the series by scores of 9-3, 11-1, and 12-2.

During the first month of the season, the Rebels were as impressive as their preseason ranking suggested. By week three of the season, they were 13-1 and had moved up the rankings to the No. 2 spot in the nation.

After a week-four victory over Alcorn State and a series win over Oral Roberts, the Rebels moved into the No. 1 spot. By March 23, the Rebels stood at 16-4, had outscored their opponents 196-83, and were averaging 9.8 runs per game.

All great stories have one thing in common — just when you think your hero knows their place in the world, something happens that changes everything. And the storybook 2022 Ole Miss baseball season was no exception.

Our talented team was riding high leading into its first home SEC series. The opponent: Tennessee. The Volunteers were also on a winning streak. In fact, some national polls had Tennessee ranked No. 1 and Ole Miss No. 2.

A clash of titans awaited Ole Miss fans. And the weekend of March 25-27, all eyes would be on Oxford-University Stadium/Swayze Field as the top two teams in the nation battled.

OLE MISS BASEBALL
OPENING WEEKEND

Students celebrate the first home run of the season after a long winter break

Ole Miss

Hudson Sapp fielding a fly ball against Memphis

5
3

54 SEC
MALONE
54

Tywone Malone points to the students after clobbering a two-run home run in the 7th inning of the February 27th game vs VCU

Peyton Chatagnier and Garrett Wood meet in a postgame ritual on the outfield grass after defeating Charleston Southern

1

McCANTS
16

TJ McCants celebrates a home run with Tim Elko and teammates in the sixth inning of the March 13th game vs Oral Roberts

Ole Miss

Peyton Chatagnier turns a double play on March 13th vs Oral Roberts

M
Rebels
5

LEFT: Mike Bianco before the ULM game; ABOVE: Tim Elko rounding third base after a home run against Oral Roberts

Peyton Chatagnier laughs as he slides into home after stealing all three bases vs Alcorn State

SEC
56

Ole Miss

A SLUMP

MARCH 25-MAY 6, 2022

ON TOP OF THE COLLEGE BASEBALL WORLD

Friday afternoon, March 25, was an idyllic day for Ole Miss baseball — sunny, cool, perfect field conditions. The Ole Miss baseball squad had been ranked No. 1 in the nation for the second straight week, and Rebel nation, rightfully, basked in the glory.

Players posed for photos with fans; kids stood in line for autographs; everyone — from fans to coaches — seemed to be having fun.

ABOVE: Lane Kiffin greeting Coach Bianco after Coach Kiffin threw the first pitch against Tennessee. In homage to the previous fall's football game, Coach Kiffin threw a golf ball.

Ole Miss Head Football Coach Lane Kiffin was scheduled to throw out the first pitch. In homage to last season's controversial Ole Miss/Tennessee football game in Knoxville, Coach Kiffin pulled out a golf ball — much to the delight of Rebel fans — and tossed it to the catcher.

Laughter, lightness, and camaraderie enveloped Swayze Field.

Until the first pitch.

A RECKONING

Tennessee dominated every facet of Game 1 (the final score was 12-1). The Volunteers were no less dominant in a 10-3 victory in Game 2. And though the Rebels kept Game 3 close, Tennessee swept the series with a 4-3 win.

The sweep propelled Tennessee to No. 1 (a spot they kept for the remainder of the season) and dropped Ole Miss to No. 10.

The Rebels stood at 2-4 in SEC play.

Ole Miss rebounded nicely the next four games, rolling past North Alabama 20-3 at home and taking two of three SEC games at Kentucky to improve to 19-8 on the season and almost even things up in SEC play at 4-5. The finale against the Wildcats was a 10-1 victory for the Rebels, and it appeared they might be back on track.

But something was awry.

The Rebels seemed lost. Most teams, by this point in the season, know who they are. They understand their strengths and weaknesses, their pitching rotation. But the Rebels were still searching.

And if the next four games were any indication, the team was in trouble.

A loss to Southern Miss in Pearl was followed by a sweep at the hands of Alabama in Oxford (the Crimson Tide did not make the NCAA Tournament). The Rebels' record stood at 19-12 overall and 4-8 in SEC games.

Ole Miss dropped to No. 25 in the national rankings.

Even after a win against Murray State at home and a series-opening victory at South Carolina, the next few games signaled that this season was still headed in the wrong direction.

The Gamecocks took the back two games of the series, and Ole Miss fell out of the national polls for the first time all season. The record stood at 21-14 and 5-10 in the SEC.

On April 19 in Oxford, the Rebels lost 13-3 to Southeast Missouri. Even the most passionate Ole Miss fans had a tough time envisioning how this team would finish strong.

STRENGTH DURING TURMOIL

Despite rough treatment by media and sportscasters, and some grumbling among the fan base about the season collapsing, the team stayed together. In the locker room, they were one. They believed in one another.

And Coach Bianco believed, too. He knew this team had too much talent, too much drive, too much spirit to quit. Sure, the team might need to make some adjustments, but no one in the Rebel locker room was ready to surrender.

FACING THE 2021 NATIONAL CHAMPIONS

Mississippi State, the college baseball national champion in 2021 and the Rebels' archrival, was the next opponent for four consecutive games. Ole Miss claimed Game 1 of the SEC series in Oxford 4-2. The Bulldogs won Game 2, 10-7 and Game 3, 7-6 in 11 innings.

In an annual non-conference game in Pearl called The Governor's Cup, Ole Miss won 5-2 against MSU. Then it was on to Arkansas for more SEC games.

In late April, the Rebels traveled to Fayetteville to face the No. 4-ranked Razorbacks. Ole Miss won the opener 4-2. Arkansas took the second game 6-3. On Sunday, May 1, Ole Miss lost a close game to the Razorbacks 4-3.

The Rebels were 24-19 overall and 7-14 in SEC play.

That dismal SEC record would be a thorn in the side of the team and coaches for the remainder of the season.

Final exams at Ole Miss began on Monday, May 2. No baseball games were scheduled during the week.

And just as finals signal the end of one semester and a fresh beginning, the Ole Miss season was about to take a turn.

And the transformation would transfix baseball fans everywhere.

ABOVE: A fan's T-shirt, also in homage to the Tennessee football game

SEC

Ole Miss

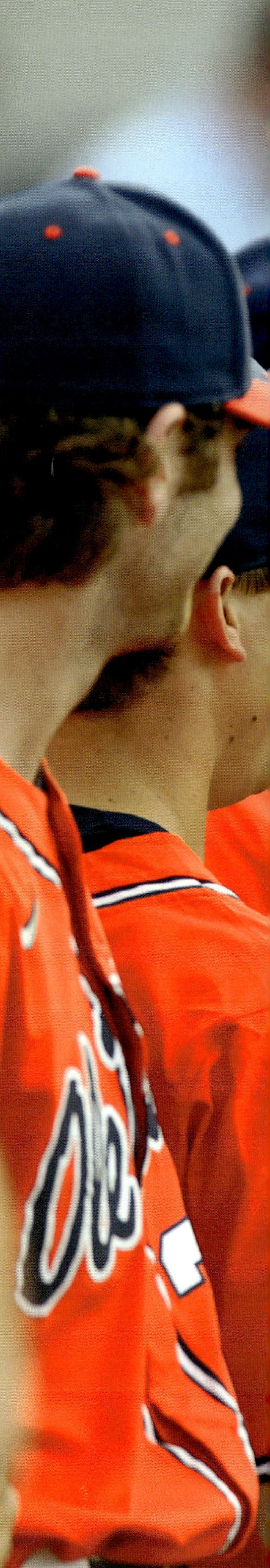

ABOVE: Peyton Chatagnier in thought; RIGHT: Country music star and former Rebel pitcher Brett Young before the MSU game

18
SEC

Knox Loposer celebrates with Peyton Chatagnier after a first-inning home run vs North Alabama

EASTON
39

Ole Miss

Ole Miss
18
Ole Miss
39
24
38

Calvin Harris celebrates with Peyton Chatagnier after a diving catch at Swayze Field

Rebels
20
A2000

Jacob Gonzales turns a double play

127A
RESTROOM

Kevin Graham ready to play for the first time after recovering from an injury

Kevin Graham watches his first post-injury home run leave the field

Ole Miss
35

Tim Elko celebrating a home run against MSU

SEC
3
44
CHATAGNIER
1
10

Rebels
22

Ole Miss
UNIVERSITY OF MISSISSIPPI
FedEx
Ole Miss

Ole Miss

RESURRECTION

MAY 6-MAY 24, 2022

The Rebels needed something to lift them out of the depths. That something was Missouri. The Tigers roared into Oxford expecting to sweep a beaten-down Ole Miss team, but the Rebels sent Missouri home with three losses.

However, there were still questions: Were the Rebels out of their slump? Or was Missouri just not very good?

PITCHERS ON A ROLL

For the fourth consecutive weekend, Dylan DeLucia had started Game 1 of an SEC series — and all four times Ole Miss won those starts. One had been a complete game 4-2 win against Mississippi State, perhaps proving to the coaches that the first-year junior college transfer could get it done for nine innings in a game. That would be key later in the season.

Mason Nichols

Against Missouri, DeLucia wasn't his best and went just four innings. But relief help from Mason Nichols, Jack Dougherty, and Brandon Johnson helped Ole Miss to a 7-5 win. In the sixth inning, Peyton Chatagnier broke a 5-5 tie with a solo homer that proved to be the winning run.

The opening win seemed to set a tone for the next few games. Ole Miss won Game 2, 8-1 as Hunter Elliott picked up his second win of the season. In the finale, the Rebels scored 10 runs in the first four innings and never looked back in a 10-2 win. Derek Diamond, with the win, and John Gaddis, with a save, took care of the Tiger batters.

At 27-19 overall and 10-14 in the SEC, the Rebels still had a long way to go, but the prospects looked brighter. And brighter still they would get.

USM & LSU

Ole Miss, as it typically does en route to LSU, stopped for a midweek, non-conference game against Southern Miss in Hattiesburg. The announced attendance of 6,346 at Pete Taylor Park/Hill Denson Field was the largest in USM home history. Ole Miss won 4-1. What no one knew at the time was that the Rebels would return for more baseball in Hattiesburg in the postseason.

Game 1 at LSU was another opening series win for DeLucia, as well as a save for Johnson, as a four-run second inning proved to be enough for a 5-3 Ole Miss victory.

In the series' second game, Tim Elko's solo home run in the first and Kevin Graham's solo homer in the second set the tone. Hayden Dunhurst launched one out with a runner aboard in the fourth, and Justin Bench's solo home run in the fifth all helped their team to an 11-1 victory. Hunter Elliott and Josh Mallitz took care of business on the mound.

On Sunday, Justin Bench took the very first pitch of the game deep to the wall for a lead-off double, and the Rebels never looked back, finishing off a sweep of LSU at Alex Box Stadium with an 8-5 win Sunday afternoon. According to the record book, it was Ole Miss' first three-game sweep at LSU.

No. 4 TEXAS A&M

The Rebels had improved to 31-19 and 13-14 and were feeling every bit as confident as it appeared. A very good fourth-ranked Texas A&M team was headed for Oxford. The Rebels were down 7-0 after an inning and a half in the opener. The hole was just too deep. The 10-5 Aggie victory brought a seven-game winning streak to an end. It appeared Game 2 might follow suit with Ole Miss trailing 3-0 after the top of the first. But the Rebels regained the magic of the previous two weekends and roared past the Aggies 14-6. In Game 3, a four-run third inning gave the Rebels a three-run lead in Saturday's series finale with Texas A&M, but the Aggies put up seven runs in the fourth and moved on to a 12-5 win.

VANDY IN THE SEC TOURNAMENT

With a record of 32-21 and an SEC record of 14-16, Ole Miss turned its attention to the SEC Tournament in Hoover, Alabama. As the No. 9 seed, Ole Miss would face the No. 8 seed, Vanderbilt. That game was on single-elimination Tuesday, and the loser of the game would go home.

Dylan DeLucia and Josh Mallitz kept the Commodore offense in check for the most part. But the Rebel bats were not up to the task on this day, and Ole Miss headed back to Oxford after a 3-1 loss to await their NCAA postseason fate.

No one knew if the Ole Miss season was over. And the Rebels would have to wait six more days — for the completion of conference championships and the NCAA Selection Show on Memorial Day Monday — to find out.

Jack Dougherty fired up after a strike out

WAITING

MAY 24-MAY 30

The Rebels practiced while they waited. That included two intrasquads Friday and Saturday, May 27 & 28, to make sure the pitchers were where they needed to be — just in case Ole Miss made the cut.

The prospects didn't look bright. D1 Baseball, Baseball America, and Perfect Game all projected brackets that did not include Ole Miss.

The team and coaches gathered in the Trehern Dugout Club at Swayze Field to watch the NCAA Selection Show on ESPN. As the show progressed, Ole Miss was passed over again and again.

In the waning moments, the ESPN broadcasters announced that the Rebels would play in the Coral Gables Regional Tournament. Everyone in the room went wild. Coach Bianco said he'd never seen anything like the ecstasy on display in the club.

The celebration drowned out what the announcers said next. Ole Miss was the last team selected for the tournament — 33rd of 33 at-large bids and the 64th invitation extended to a field of 64.

The Rebels — who were not ranked nationally, who had a losing conference record, and who got knocked out in the first round of the SEC tournament, were in . . . by the narrowest of margins.

Coca-Cola
Ole Miss
Rebels
12
Ole Miss
Ole Miss

Coca-Cola
Ole Miss
Rebels

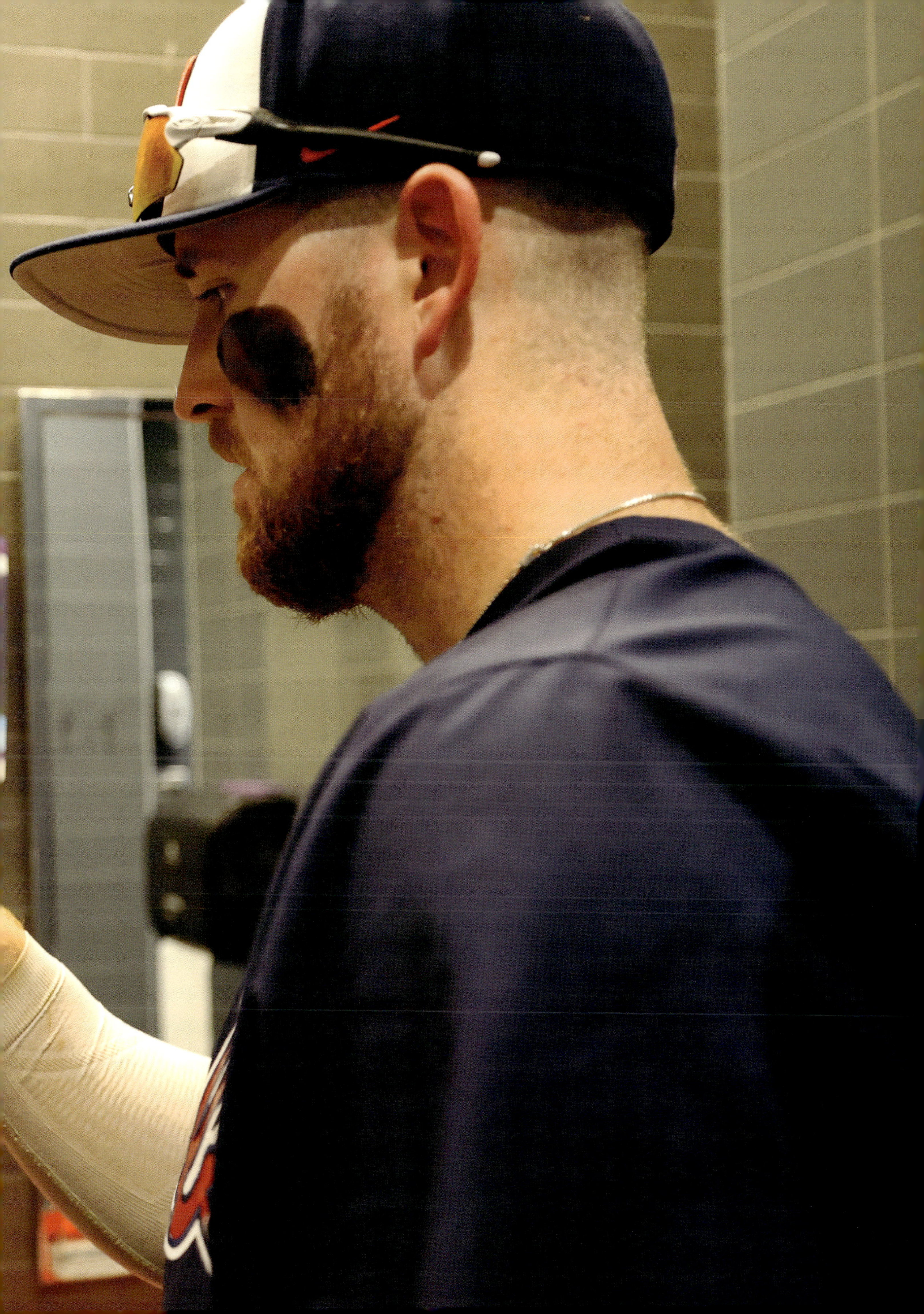

40

EASTON
Rebels
35

Dylan DeLucia's complete game against MSU

26

Ole Miss
13

After losing to Vandy in the SEC tournament in Hoover, all the Rebels could do was wait. They were not ranked nationally; they had a losing conference record, and they got knocked out in the first round of the SEC tournament. The NCAA selection committee did pick Ole Miss to play in the postseason tournament. The Rebels were the No. 64 pick out of 64 teams.

Ole Miss
44

CORAL GABLES REGIONAL

JUNE 4-6, 2022

GAME 1, JUNE 4

The cheers from players and coaches — or maybe those were sighs of relief — could be heard as far away as Miami when the Rebels were selected as the third seed in the Coral Gables Regional. Ole Miss was the last at-large team selected — the last team selected for the tournament.

As Mike Bianco would say on several occasions in the postseason, the Rebels had been running uphill for weeks trying to get into the NCAA Tournament. But now they were 0-0 and running on an even field again.

The 32-22 Rebels faced second-seeded Arizona, 37-23, on the first day of the Regional, which was postponed from its scheduled Friday until Saturday because of a tropical system that passed through the area. Ole Miss and Arizona played until early Sunday morning at Alex Rodriguez Park on Mark Light Field, with the Rebels winning 7-4.

Dylan DeLucia had a career-high 12 strikeouts before exiting in the seventh inning with the game tied 4-4. Josh Mallitz came in and followed with five strikeouts in the seventh and eighth. Brandon Johnson tallied three more strikeouts to close it out in the ninth and give Ole Miss 20 strikeouts on the night, the most in program history in postseason play and just one shy of the Rebels' single-game school record.

Offensively, Peyton Chatagnier was spectacular, going 3-for-4 with four RBIs, including a game-tying home run in the seventh and a bases-loaded, three-run double in the eighth to give the Rebels the lead they would not relinquish.

Arizona's Chase Davis had opened the scoring with a leadoff home run to left field in the second inning. Two batters later, Garen Caulfield sent a ball over the right field fence for another solo shot.

The Wildcats' lead would last until the fourth when Jacob Gonzalez, following a Justin Bench leadoff single, crushed a no-doubter just inside the right field foul pole to tie the game 2-2.

After Arizona scored two runs in the bottom of the sixth, the Rebels answered in a hurry. With Kemp Alderman on first after a leadoff single in the top of the seventh, Chatagnier sent a ball out of the park to tie it 4-4.

In the eighth, walks to Gonzalez, Tim Elko and Alderman loaded the bases, and Chatagnier cleared them, sending a double down the left field line to make it 7-4.

Arizona threatened in the bottom of the ninth, with runners on second and third and no outs. With the tying run at the plate, Johnson struck out three straight Wildcats to give Ole Miss the victory to open NCAA Tournament play.

Johnson's determination to close it out and focus on winning set the tone for the Rebels in the postseason.

GAME 2, JUNE 5

On Sunday afternoon, top-seeded Miami and Ole Miss faced off in a winners' bracket game — a game that turned out to be a pitching and defensive battle.

True freshman Hunter Elliott looked anything but a rookie as he pitched five innings with just one run allowed, striking out eight. Fellow freshman Mason Nichols retired all seven batters he faced before handing the ball to Brandon Johnson, who locked up his eleventh save of the season, and second in as many days.

The Rebels, who in this game were the home team, held the Hurricanes to a season-low four hits, striking out 14.

Coming through when he was needed, captain Tim Elko led the charge and reached all four times at the plate, going 2-for-2 with a pair of walks and the game's biggest knock.

Elliott and Miami starter Carson Palmquist, both left-handers, traded zeroes into the middle innings, when the Hurricanes finally broke through in the sixth. Following a walk and a wild pitch, Hayden Leatherwood was unable to hang onto a liner to right field, putting runners at the corners with nobody out. That brought Mason Nichols out of the bullpen, and the true freshman limited the damage, surrendering only one run on a sacrifice fly.

Down 1-0, Ole Miss looked set to respond, putting two in scoring position on Gonzalez's leadoff single, Elko's walk, and a wild pitch. However, the Rebels left the bases loaded with three strikeouts.

While an opportunity didn't materialize in the sixth, it

did in the seventh as the Rebels put together a two-out rally. After Bench and Gonzalez notched back-to-back singles, Elko sent a ball into the right-center gap to bring both home, and a 1-0 deficit became a 2-1 advantage.

With the lead in hand, Nichols, who picked up his first collegiate win, got the first out of the eighth inning, and from there it was Johnson who got the final two outs of the eighth.

A one-out double in the top of the ninth put the tying run on for the Hurricanes. With his back against the wall, Johnson again produced, striking out back-to-back Miami batters to send the Rebels into the Regional final.

GAME 3, JUNE 6

After Arizona eliminated Miami in Monday's first game, the Wildcats immediately faced an Ole Miss team that had not played since the previous afternoon.

Arizona pitching was limited. When Ole Miss put up a five spot in the top of the fifth to lead 10-5, this one was basically over.

The final score was 22-6, and the Rebels were on their way to a Super Regional.

Regional MVP Tim Elko posted astonishing numbers on the weekend with a .778 batting average, seven hits, three doubles, three home runs, seven RBIs, a 2.111 slugging percentage, and a .857 on-base percentage.

Also on the all-tournament team was Peyton Chatagnier, who batted .538 with five extra base hits and a team-high 10 RBIs, as well as Jacob Gonzalez, Hunter Elliott and Brandon Johnson.

Like they had all weekend, Elko and Chatagnier led the way for the Rebels. Elko reached and scored all six times at the plate, tying the single-game runs record while hitting three home runs and posting five RBIs. Chatagnier was 4-for-6, bringing home six runs and scoring two himself.

Jack Dougherty earned the win out of the bullpen, allowing two hits and a pair of walks over 2.1 innings. On the weekend in three games, the Rebel bullpen did not allow a single earned run over 12.1 innings.

Elko got the party started in the first inning, hammering a two-run shot the other way following Jacob Gonzalez's walk. The Wildcats responded in kind, though, with Tanner O'Tremba tying the game with a two-run blast of his own.

Chatagnier continued to light it up in regional play, recapturing the lead for Ole Miss in the second, pulling a two-run homer a few feet inside of the foul pole, making it 4-2 Rebels.

Ahead 10-5, Ole Miss scored eight runs in the sixth inning, highlighted by back-to-back two-run doubles from Chatagnier and Calvin Harris.

In the seventh inning, Elko hit his third homer of the game. It was the first time in the slugger's prolific career he had hit three round-trippers in the same game, and the first time ever a Rebel has accomplished the feat in an NCAA Tournament game.

Elko's third homer gave the Rebel captain the Ole Miss single-season home run record with 22 on the year.

After Arizona scored on an RBI single in the seventh, Ole Miss put the finishing touches on in the ninth. Elko and Ben Van Cleve got on through a single and double, with Elko coming around on Alderman's infield single. Chatagnier then put the cherry on top, rocketing a double to right-center, scoring Van Cleve and Alderman to bring the score to its resting place.

Derek Diamond had gotten the start, but Jack Dougherty got the win. John Gaddis also pitched, and it was Jack Washburn out of the bullpen in the ninth who finished things up.

The Rebels stood at 35-22 on the season.

Next stop? The Super Regional in Hattiesburg.

Dylan DeLucia in the dugout before starting against Arizona in the Coral Gables Regional

54 ALL-AMERI
ANES
Rebels
44

Brandon Johnson celebrating a win in Coral Gables

CHATAGNIER
1
Rebels
8
23

Rebels
40

SEC
GRADUATE
Rebel

WOOD
40

Justin Bench crossing the plate against Miami in Coral Gables

M
Rebels
8

Peyton Chatagnier and third-base coach Mike Clement after a home run against Arizona in Coral Gables

M
Ole Miss
1

Jacob Gonzalez making a play at shortstop against Arizona in Coral Gables

M
Miss
1

Ole Miss
12

LEFT: Kemp Alderman pointing to the heavens against Arizona in Coral Gables;
ABOVE: Jack Dougherty stares down an Arizona hitter after a strikeout

ALDERMAN
12

Kemp Alderman putting the ball in flight during Game 3 of the Coral Gables Regional

HATTIESBURG SUPER REGIONAL

JUNE 11-12, 2022

Ole Miss returned home from Miami on June 7 two wins away from the College World Series. The Rebels would play those Super Regional games on the road — but it would still be a Mississippi field. The matchup was scheduled against No. 10 Southern Miss in Hattiesburg.

Southern Miss and Ole Miss typically play two baseball games in the regular season. In the two 2022 matchups, they had split the games.

The programs are quite familiar with each other. So are the head coaches — Ole Miss head coach Mike Bianco and USM head coach Scott Berry.

"We've talked all week how cool it is to have a Super Regional with two teams in our state going at it," Bianco said the day before the first game. "Scott and his program have had a tremendous year and certainly are super deserving to host a Super Regional. We didn't have a super year, but we've played well at the end. We're excited to be here and to still be playing."

"First of all," said Berry, who recently completed his thirteenth season as head coach at USM, "I'd like to congratulate Mike and his team on making it to the Super Regional. Big fan of his. When he came to Mississippi as the head coach at Ole Miss in 2000, that's when Coach (Corky) Palmer asked me to come be the assistant at Southern Miss. We've been able to develop a really nice relationship and a competitive relationship over those years. Very proud of our squad to make it to this level."

GAME 1, JUNE 11

On a blistering hot sunny day in the Deep South for Game 1 of the Super Regional, the Rebels jumped out to a 3-0 lead. The top of the sixth inning started innocently enough with a walk of the Rebels' Peyton Chatagnier. Seven runs later in that same inning, Ole Miss was ahead 10-0.

The Rebels beat Southern Miss 10-0 (their first shutout victory of the season) but more importantly, the Rebels held a 1-0 lead in the best of three series at Pete Taylor Park/Hill Denson Field.

Rebel starting pitcher Dylan DeLucia was nothing short of magnificent. DeLucia allowed no runs through five and a third innings on 108 pitches, with nine strikeouts and just four hits. He didn't allow a free pass until back-to-back walks in the fifth.

Jack Dougherty came in to relieve DeLucia after five and two-thirds and kept the Golden Eagles at bay for his second save of the season. Over the final 3.1 innings, Dougherty struck out one batter but let his defense do its work, and no Golden Eagle reached base with 10 batters faced.

Tim Elko led the Rebel offense, going 2-for-5 with three RBI. Calvin Harris also had a two-hit day, and Kevin Graham had a two-RBI game.

One win away from Omaha.

GAME 2, JUNE 12

Ole Miss starter Hunter Elliott was sensational, pitching seven and a third innings with 10 strikeouts and only three hits. He faced only 25 batters, and in one stretch of the contest retired 16 straight.

The Rebels scored three runs in the fifth inning to take a lead they never relinquished. A Jacob Gonzalez RBI single scored Calvin Harris, who had reached on a single. Justin Bench, who got on with a double, later scored on a passed ball from USM starter Tanner Hall. Gonzalez scored on a single by Kevin Graham.

Hayden Dunhurst led off the sixth with a base hit and later scored on a Bench single. That made the score 4-0, and things were about to get interesting in the top of the eighth.

In the eighth inning with his team leading 4-0, Elliott gave up a single to Golden Eagle Slade Wilks. After one out, Gabe Montenegro singled. At that point, Elliott's superb day was done. Josh Mallitz came in and took care of business, but it got a bit shaky for a few moments.

USM's Reece Ewing walked to load the bases with two outs, but Carson Paetow flew out to shortstop Peyton Chatagnier, and there was no damage. Ole Miss, the designated home team in Game 2, had three outs to go.

Then in the bottom of the eighth, TJ McCants, who had not played recently due to injury, sent one out of the yard for late-inning insurance for the Rebels. It was 5-0.

Mallitz finished the game and got those outs in the top of the ninth.

Ole Miss had its second shutout of the year.

It was time to go to Omaha.

SEC
GRADUATE

Mike Bianco and USM
head coach Scott Berry

USM
adidas
USM
40

Hunter Elliott warming up pregame at the Hattiesburg Super Regional as Ole Miss assistant coach Carl Lafferty watches

Garrett Wood celebrating a base hit in the Hattiesburg Super Regional

Tim Elko checks on Hayden Dunhurst after the 7th inning of a scorching game where temperatures registered as high as 140 degrees on the Southern Miss turf

Rebels
35
ELKO
SEC

MURRELL
18

TJ McCants celebrating with teammates in Game 2 of the Hattiesburg Super Regional

The final out is recorded in Hattiesburg, sending the Rebels to Omaha for the first time since 2014

SEC

SEC

KIMBRELL

Rebels
56
Rebels
2
Rebels
20
Rebels
4
Rebels
26
Rebels
17
Rebels
Rebels
Rebels

EAT MOR FOWL
Ole Miss
6 ROW 17 SEAT 22

COLLEGE WORLD SERIES

OMAHA ■ JUNE 18--26, 2022

The Rebels were back.

It had been eight years — the 2014 season — since Ole Miss appeared in Omaha for the College World Series. And it was the school's sixth appearance — three under Coach Tom Swayze, one under Coach Jake Gibbs, and now, two under Coach Mike Bianco.

If history repeated itself, the Rebels would be headed back to Oxford before the championship series.

In a double elimination tournament, a lot has to go right for a team to win the title, and the baseball gods need to shine some light along the way.

But things would be different in 2022.

GAME ONE: AUBURN, JUNE 18

Game One was against a familiar foe, Southeastern Conference Western Division rival Auburn. In the first weekend in March, the Rebels won two of three games on the road. But Auburn had a better regular season and hosted an NCAA Regional. Ole Miss, however, was getting hot.

Dylan DeLucia started the game on a masterful note. The Rebel ace went 7.2 innings, allowing one run on four hits with ten strikeouts. DeLucia retired the first 14 Tiger batters.

The top of the first inning, before Auburn even came up to bat, got things rolling for the Rebels and set the tone in this game.

A two-out single by Tim Elko was followed by a Kevin Graham double to the left field corner to put runners in scoring position. On a 2-2 count, Kemp Alderman singled to right and moved to second on a throwing error by Auburn third baseman Blake Rambusch. Both Elko and Graham scored.

The Rebels continued their hot streak. They had come to play.

As DeLucia basically cruised, Ole Miss was ready to add another run soon. In the third inning the Rebels increased their lead to 3-0 on a solo home run by Graham, who would end up with three hits in the game. There were two outs when Graham knocked it out of the park, as the Rebels continued to take advantage of effective two-out hitting.

In the sixth, Ole Miss added two more. Alderman led off the top of the sixth with a single. Hayden Dunhurst was then hit by a Joseph Gonzalez pitch, and the Auburn starter's night was done.

The final score of the final game of the opening weekend of the College World Series was Ole Miss 5, Auburn 1. The Rebels were again dominant on the mound and in the field. Ole Miss also out hit the Tigers 11-4 in the game.

But up next for Ole Miss was another familiar foe — and yet another team from the SEC West.

Only this opponent is considered a much bigger baseball rival for the Rebels than Auburn. And they'd had the upper hand in recent years.

GAME TWO: ARKANSAS, JUNE 20

Of the seven teams Ole Miss could potentially face during the College World Series, one stood out as the likely team to block the Rebels' path to a national championship — Arkansas.

No two programs in the SEC are more familiar with one another. The head coaches' teams have played so often on the field that it's believed they have faced each other more than any two head coaches in SEC baseball history. This game would be their 72nd meeting.

Mike Bianco, in 22 seasons at Ole Miss, has the third most wins in SEC history; Dave Van Horn, at Arkansas for 20 years, ranks fifth.

The Rebels had lost two of three games to Arkansas in Fayetteville during the regular season series. So how would things unfold on the game's biggest stage?

This one would turn out to be all Ole Miss.

The Rebels scored two runs in each of the first three innings, which proved to ultimately be enough as they beat Arkansas 13-5 to remain unbeaten in the NCAA Tournament.

Freshman All-American Hunter Elliott, sensational on the mound in recent weeks, continued to be just that. Elliott started and pitched six and a third innings, finishing with only one earned run on six hits with four strikeouts and two walks. He threw 100 pitches.

The Ole Miss bats were hot. In the second inning, Elko strolled to the plate with two outs, and moments later sent a 2-2 pitch out of the park to deep left, measured at 416 feet from home plate. The Rebels led 4-1.

Few could have predicted the outcome to be so one-sided, but in baseball almost anything is possible. Ole Miss outhit Arkansas 13-8. Justin Bench had four hits in the contest, while Calvin Harris had three. Harris with four RBI and Elko with three, as well as two RBI each from Bench and Kevin Graham, took care of much of the scoring for the Rebels.

There are certain benchmarks in the CWS a team wants to reach as the tournament progresses. One of those is to be 2-0. It puts a team in the driver's seat.

That's where Ole Miss found itself.

Ole Miss had established itself as one of the teams to beat — maybe the most formidable foe remaining in the tournament. Texas and Stanford had already been eliminated with two losses each. There were six teams left: Oklahoma, also 2-0, along with Arkansas, Notre Dame, Texas A&M, Auburn, and Ole Miss.

By the time Ole Miss would play again, on Wednesday, two more teams would be eliminated: Auburn and Notre Dame.

The Rebels' foe in that Wednesday game? Arkansas.

Again.

GAME THREE: ARKANSAS, JUNE 22

For three weeks all had been well for Ole Miss. A loss was almost unthinkable. But this was baseball, and two great teams were meeting again.

The game turned out to be a battle of pitchers.

Ole Miss had a chance to win. In the bottom of the ninth inning, trailing 3-1, the Rebels had the bases loaded and no outs. But the Rebels only managed to score one run. The Razorbacks won 3-2.

Ole Miss and Arkansas would play the next day. It was the third game in a row between the two rivals— and the sixth contest during the 2022 season.

But this one would be the biggest of them all.

GAME FOUR: ARKANSAS, JUNE 23

Ole Miss and Arkansas were meeting for the third time in four days.

The winner would advance to the championship series against Oklahoma. The loser's season would be over.

The two SEC Western Division foes were waging war once again, and this time more was on the line than any other meeting in the history of the series.

One team would make history.

And thanks to Ole Miss pitcher Dylan DeLucia, it would be Ole Miss.

Sportswriters called DeLucia's performance "a masterpiece."

The junior right-hander, in his first season at Ole Miss (he played for two years at Northwest Florida State College), pitched a complete game to extend the Rebels' season and deliver them into the championship series.

DeLucia struck out seven Razorbacks and allowed only four hits, facing 32 Hogs and not allowing a free pass in the 2-0 victory. He simply let his defense do its job.

It was the performance the Rebels needed, leaving the bullpen fully stocked for the final series. DeLucia's shutout was the first by an SEC pitcher at the College World Series since LSU's Brett Laxton in 1993.

"What a great pitchers' duel," said Arkansas head coach Dave Van Horn. "Both pitchers gave it everything they had."

"Just wow," said Ole Miss head coach Mike Bianco. "Another really great baseball game by both teams. Another great pitching performance by both clubs. The story of the day was Dylan (DeLucia). A legendary performance."

Ole Miss and Oklahoma had Friday off before the start of the championship series on Saturday night.

The weekend ahead was all about winning a national championship and hoisting the hardware that accompanies it.

GAME FIVE: OKLAHOMA, JUNE 25

"It's going to be a good series between (Ole Miss) and Oklahoma," said Razorbacks head coach Dave Van Horn. "Oklahoma is going to be rested and have all their arms loaded and ready to go. But the way Ole Miss has been playing down the stretch, it might not matter."

The Sooners entered the weekend 3-0 in the College World Series, while Ole Miss was 3-1. Friday, June 24, was an off day reserved for a press conference for Rebels and Sooners players and coaches, and the last practices of the season.

More Ole Miss fans continued to roll toward Nebraska. By game time on Saturday night, Charles Schwab Field resembled a home game at Oxford-University Stadium/Swayze Field. Many of them held signs that read, "Don't Let the Rebs Get Hot."

And that is exactly what happened.

Ole Miss came out swinging in its 10-3 victory against Oklahoma in the championship series opener.

Before it was over, the Rebels had 16 hits with four home runs, including back-to-back-to-back round-trippers that put the game out of reach in the eighth inning.

But it wasn't just offense. Rebel pitchers — starter Jack Dougherty and relievers Mason Nichols and Josh Mallitz — were totally in command of the mound and kept a potent Oklahoma offense down most of the night.

The Rebels made some CWS history with three straight home runs in the eighth inning. TJ McCants launched one into the Ole Miss bullpen, and the Rebels led 6-2. Calvin Harris sent one 430 feet to center and the score was 7-2. Justin Bench completed the trifecta, putting one in the left field stands for the first back-to-back-to-back home runs at the College World Series since it moved to Charles Schwab Field in 2011, and the first in CWS history since LSU accomplished the feat in 1998.

The Rebels and Sooners headed to a Sunday afternoon game with Ole Miss needing just one more win to claim the title.

GAME SIX: OKLAHOMA, JUNE 26

Ole Miss and Oklahoma met in game two of the national championship series on a bright, sunny, hot, Sunday in the middle of America in a stadium just inside Nebraska across the Missouri River from Iowa.

Charles Schwab Field was again packed with nearly 26,000 fans, and estimates were pretty consistent that more than 20,000 of them were Rebel fans. Some said the crowd and noise and atmosphere felt more like a college football game.

It certainly showed the nation that Ole Miss fans do love their teams. And this would turn out to be a special day in the history of Rebel baseball.

In the final game of the college baseball season, the contest was scoreless through the top of the fifth inning as Ole Miss starter Hunter Elliott and Cade Horton of Oklahoma were pitching effectively for their respective teams.

Just minutes into the sixth inning, an obstruction call at first base erased a Sooner run.

And at the bottom of the sixth, a one-out solo home run by Jacob Gonzalez to right center gave the Rebels a 1-0 lead.

But after Gonzalez's homer, things remained interesting the rest of the way. The Sooners scored two runs with two outs in the seventh and chased Elliott from the game. Before the inning was over, both Mason Nichols and John Gaddis had pitched for the Rebels, and the Sooners led 2-1.

In the bottom of the eighth inning, Ole Miss scored three runs off of All-American closer Michael Trevin to take a 4-2 lead. The crowd of Rebel supporters were whipped into a frenzy. They could sense a national championship was at hand.

When it was over, veteran Rebel play-by-play man David Kellum announced, *The Ole Miss Rebels are national champions!* His words reverberated across Rebel Nation.

The Rebels poured out of the dugout and onto the field for a championship dogpile.

Ole Miss had managed six hits to only three for Oklahoma, and they had doubled the Sooners with a 4-2 final score as well.

The contest was played before a crowd announced at 25,972. The celebration and awards ceremony on the field lasted for more than an hour.

The Rebels' Dylan DeLucia was named Outstanding Player of the 2022 College World Series. DeLucia was joined on the CWS all-tournament team by his teammates Tim Elko, Justin Bench, Calvin Harris, Kevin Graham and Kemp Alderman.

The Rebels finished the season 42-23, winning 10 of 11 games during a sensational run through the NCAA postseason. It is the first baseball national championship in program history.

The fans stayed in the stands for more than an hour after the game ended.

That euphoria continues today.

"Here in Omaha, the Rebels have not lacked for support and encouragement. Probably 20,000 Ole Miss fans were present at Charles Schwab Field, often standing, screaming and waving towels at all the right moments. The crowd fed off the Rebels; the Rebels fed off the crowd. Afterward, players circled the field, high-fiving joyous fans. There were Ole Miss fans reaching over one another to reach over the fence in every section of the stadium. Nearly an hour after the game had ended, Ole Miss fans still stood and cheered."

RICK CLEVELAND
reporting for *Mississippi Today* from Omaha

REBEL NATION

More than 20,000 Ole Miss fans attended each of the six games in Omaha. It left an impression on the city, fans from other universities, and a national television audience.

Kevin Culjat, owner of Rocco's Pizza and Cantina (home of the famous jello shot competition) said, "I think I can speak for everyone here, every business around this ballpark, when I say that we've never seen anything like what we have seen from the teams this week, but especially Ole Miss fans." Culjat went on to say that he was happy his newfound Rebel friends won the national championship, but he'd wished the finals would have gone to three games so Omaha's economy might have one more day of powder-blue spending.

Ole Miss team captain, Tim Elko, also chimed in.

"Yeah, I would say there were probably 20,000 Rebels there. It was an amazing environment. Super fun to play in. Just having all that support, it makes it a lot of fun to play."

The *Clarion-Ledger* reported, "the 2022 College World Series set a new attendance record with 366,105 fans over 15 games in Omaha. That eclipsed the record of 361,711 fans set in 2021 when cross-state rival Mississippi State came out on top. Sunday's crowd of 25,972 was 1,467 over stadium capacity and the biggest crowd in a College World Series finals game since 2017. That total included 20,000-plus Rebels fans, demonstrating that no one supports their college baseball teams like fans from Mississippi."

Chris Coghlan making a surprise visit before the Auburn game in Omaha

Mike Bianco greeting fans at
Charles Schwab Field in Omaha

Ole Miss

EASTON
NCAA

Jacob Gonzalez warming up before batting at the College World Series

ELKO
25
25 SEC

GADDIS
WASHBURN
56
MURRELL
18
DIAMOND
2

LEFT: Cheering on teammates in Omaha;
TOP: A happy Dylan DeLucia;
MIDDLE: Josh Mallitz pumped on the mound;
BOTTOM: A laugh at Peyton Manning's expense

Hunter Elliott in the bullpen

M

NCAA
COLLEGE
Ole Miss
EASTON

Rebels staying loose pregame in the locker room

33
SEC
GRADUATE

Kemp Alderman celebrating with Justin Bench and Ben Van Cleve against Arkansas in Omaha

College Station 830mi
South Bend
Oxford 719 mi.
AUBURN 996mi.
472mi
AUSTin 843mi

NCAA
MEN'S
COLLEGE
WORLD SERIES
OMAHA
OLE MISS
OUT
Ole Miss

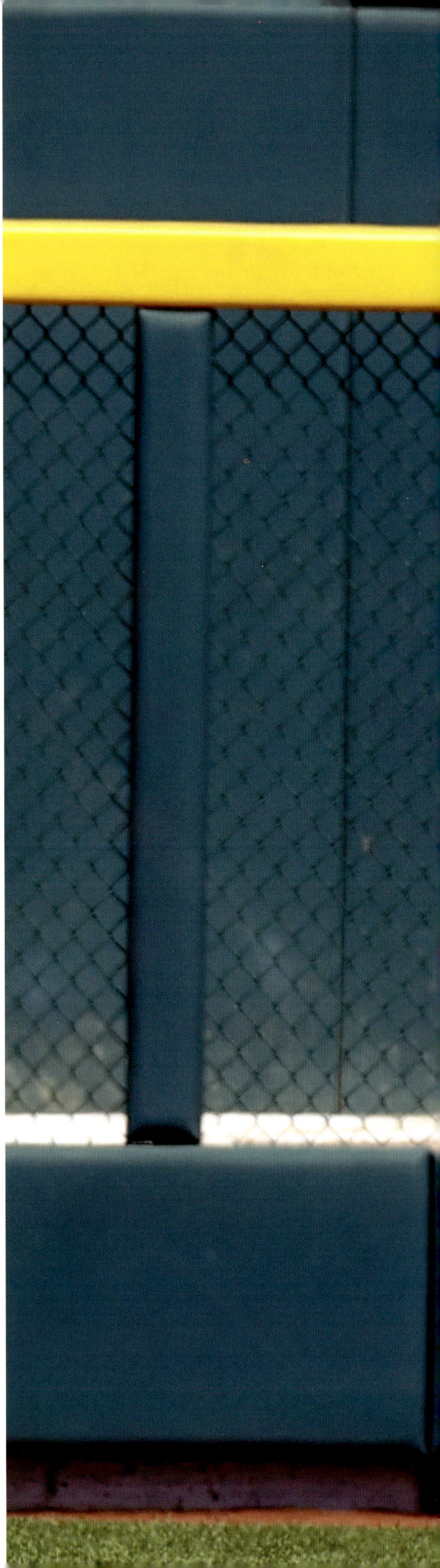

Kevin Graham making a highlight-reel catch in left field

Dylan DeLucia pitched one of the greatest complete games in Ole Miss history against Arkansas on June 23, 2022. DeLucia struck out seven Razorbacks and allowed only four hits, facing 32 Hogs and not allowing a free pass in the contest. The win propelled the Rebels into the championship series against Oklahoma.

Rebels
44

VAN CLEVE
33

MCWS
MCWS
SEC
NCAA
DIRT

GREAT PLAINS GRILL
NCAA.com
Rebels
8
Rebels
Rebels
16
Rebels
35

Ole Miss became the first team since LSU (in 1998) to hit back-to-back-to-back home runs in the CWS final after the 8th-inning swings of TJ McCants, Calvin Harris, and Justin Bench

M
EASTON
Rebels
7
EASTON

NCAA
2022 DIVISION I
NATIONAL
SEC
GRADUATE
I AM SECOND
Super Hen

M
C
Rebels
25
56

NCAA
NATIONAL CHAMPION
Ole Miss

CHAMPIONSHIP CELEBRATION

JUNE 26-29, 2022 ■ OXFORD & OLE MISS

After landing in Tupelo, Oxford and Ole Miss came out in full force to welcome the Rebels home — and for a celebration parade through town, ending with a ceremony at Swayze Field.

NATIONAL CHAMPION
VA
RVCA

Hunter Elliott carrying the national championship trophy through the Walk of Champions on the Ole Miss campus the day after victory in Omaha

Dylan DeLucia with the national championship trophy in the Grove

Double decker bus parade
through downtown Oxford

16
41

22
DOUBLE
DECKER
City of Oxford

2022 NATIONAL CHAMPION ROSTER

1 • Peyton Chatagnier
Jr. • IF• 2L
Cypress, Texas
Cy-Fair

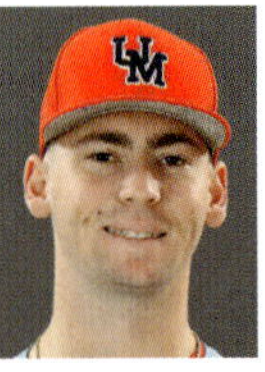
2 • Derek Diamond
Jr. • RHP• 2L
Ramona, Calif.
Ramona

3 • Hudson Sapp
R-Fr. • OF • RS
Dawsonville, Ga.
Dawson County

4 • Knox Loposer
Sr. • C • 3L
Madison, Miss.
Jackson Prep

6 • Reagan Burford
So. • IF • JC
Germantown, Tenn.
Northwest Florida State

7 • Jacob Gonzalez
So. • IF • 1L
Glendora, Calif.
Glendora

8 • Justin Bench
Sr. • IF/OF • 3L
Redington Beach, Fla.
Calvary Christian

9 • Hayden Leatherwood
Sr. • OF • 2L
Collierville, Tenn.
Northwest Mississippi CC

12 • Kemp Alderman
Fr. • OF/IF/C • HS
Decatur, Miss.
Newton County Academy

13 • Hayden Dunhurst
Jr. • C • 2L
Carriere, Miss.
Pearl River Central

14 • Tim Simay
Fr. • IF • HS
Hoschton, Ga.
Mill Creek

16 • TJ McCants
So. • IF/OF • 1L
Cantonment, Fla.
Pensacola Catholic

17 • John Kramer
Fr. • OF • HS
Wildwood, Mo.
Lafayette

18 • Mitch Murrell
Jr. • RHP • 2L
Ocean Springs, Miss.
Ocean Springs

19 • Matt Parenteau
Jr. • RHP • JC
Carmel, Ind.
Parkland College

20 • Calvin Harris
So. • C/INF • 1L
Peosta, Iowa
Western Dubuque

21 • Drew McDaniel
Jr. • RHP • 2L
Lafayette, La.
Saint Thomas More

22 • Max Cioffi
Sr. • RHP • 4L
Chicago, Ill.
Saint Patrick

23 • Josh Mallitz
So. • RHP • 1L
Tampa, Fla.
Tampa Jesuit

24 • Jackson Kimbrell
Jr. • LHP • 2L
Birmingham, Ala.
Oak Mountain

25 • Tim Elko
Sr. • IF/OF • 4L
Lutz, Fla.
Hillsborough

26 • Hunter Elliott
Fr. • LHP • HS
Tupelo, Miss.
Tupelo

27 • John Gaddis
Sr. • RHP • TR
Corpus Christi, Texas
Texas A&M - Corpus Christi

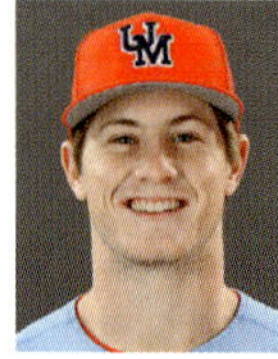
28 • Banks Tolley
Jr. • OF • JC
Madison, Miss.
Meridian CC

31 • Luke Ellis
Fr. • LHP • HS
Somerville, Tenn.
St. Benedict at Auburndale

32 • Noah Magee
Jr. • RHP • JC
Mount Olive, Miss.
Hinds CC

33 • Ben Van Cleve
Sr. • IF • 2L
Indianola, Miss.
Northwest Mississippi CC

34 • Riley Maddox
Fr. • RHP • HS
Pearl, Miss.
Jackson Prep

35 • Kevin Graham
Sr. • IF/OF • 3L
O'Fallon, Mo.
Westminster Christian

37 • Brandon Johnson
Sr. • RHP • 1L
Cottondale, Ala.
Columbia State CC

38 • Logan Savell
Jr. • RHP • 2L
Madison, Miss.
Madison Central HS

39 • Jack Dougherty
So. • RHP • 1L
Collierville, Tenn.
Collierville

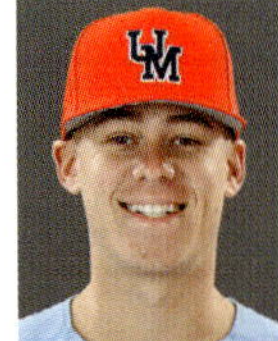
40 • Garrett Wood
Sr. • IF • 1L
Claremore, Okla.
Johnson County CC

43 • Cole Baker
Jr. • RHP • 2L
Hoover, Ala.
Hoover

44 • Dylan DeLucia
Jr. • RHP • JC
Port Orange, Fla.
Northwest Florida State

45 • Mason Nichols
Fr. • RHP • HS
Jackson, Miss.
Jackson Prep

46 • Brayden Jones
Fr. • RHP • HS
Madison, Miss.
Madison-Ridgeland Academy

50 • Blake McGehee
Fr. • RHP • HS
Tioga, La.
Tioga

54 • Tywone Malone
Fr. • IF • HS
Jamesburg, N.J.
Bergen Catholic

55 • Wes Burton
Jr. • RHP • 2L
Santa Monica, Calif.
Windward School

56 • Jack Washburn
Jr. • RHP • TR
Webster, Wisc.
Oregon State

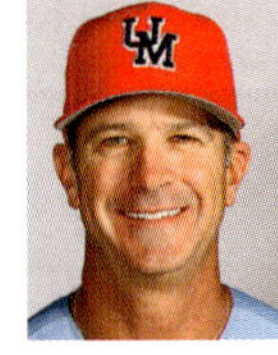
5 • Mike Bianco
Head Coach
21st Season

15 • Carl Lafferty
Assistant Coach
15th Season

30 • Mike Clement
Assistant Coach
7th Season

36 • Chris Cleary
Volunteer Assistant Coach
3rd Season

FINAL 2022 NCAA NATIONAL RANKINGS*

RANK	SCHOOL	RECORD	PREVIOUS RANK
1	Ole Miss	42-23	NR
2	Oklahoma	45-24	9
3	Texas A&M	44-20	5
4	Arkansas	46-21	23
5	Stanford	47-18	2
6	Notre Dame	41-17	17
7	Auburn	43-22	25
8	Texas	47-22	16
9	Tennessee	57-9	1
10	Oregon State	48-18	3
11	Virginia Tech	45-14	4
12	Louisville	42-21-1	8
13	East Carolina	46-21	10
14	North Carolina	42-22	11
15	Southern Miss	47-19	15
16	Connecticut	50-16	NR
17	Oklahoma State	42-22	6
18	Maryland	48-14	12
19	Texas State	47-14	13
20	Miami	40-20	7
21	Florida	42-24	18
22	UCLA	40-24	19
23	TCU	38-22	22
24	Texas Tech	39-22	24
25	LSU	40-22	NR

* Final 2022 D1Baseball.com poll

charles SCHWAB
field
OMAHA
Ole Miss
CHAMPIONS
1 2 3 4 5 6 7 8 9 10 R H E
OKLAHOMA 0 0 0 0 0 0 2 0 0 2 3 0
OLE MISS 0 0 0 0 0 1 0 3 4 6 0
AT BAT BALL 0 STRIKE 0 OUT 0 5:52

NCAA
NATIONAL CHAMPION
Ole Miss
CHAMPIONS
REBELS